The Way of the Child Jesus

Our Model of Perfection

The Way of the Child Jesus

Our Model of Perfection

By Madame Jeanne de la Mothe Guyon (1648-1717)

Original Illustrations from *Divine Love* by D'Othon Vaenius (1556-1629)

Introduction and Translation by Nancy Carol James, PhD

Copyright © 2015 by
Nancy Carol James

Madame Guyon Foundation
2324 N Quantico
Arlington, Virginia 22205

All rights reserved
Printed in the United States of America

ISBN: 978-0-9861-9710-9 (paperback)

Table of Contents

Introduction	7
Dedication to the Child Jesus	13
Chapter One Jesus Welcomes Us All	17
Chapter Two Entering into the Way	25
Chapter Three The Imitation of the Child Jesus' Interior	33
Chapter Four The Interior Purification by Penitence	37
Chapter Five The Reception of the Divine Character Within	47
Chapter Six Everyone Should Pray	55
Chapter Seven Beginning, Advanced, and Passive Prayer	67
Chapter Eight Praying Freely with Affection	81
Chapter Nine The Advantages and Ease of Abandonment	91
Chapter Ten The Exterior of the Childhood of Jesus	103
Chapter Eleven The Character of the Children Of the Holy Family	111
Chapter Twelve Spiritual Exercises to Help the Exterior	119
Chapter Thirteen The Physical Works of Mercy	127
Chapter Fourteen The Spiritual Works of Mercy	133
Selected Bibliography	145

Introduction

By Nancy Carol James, PhD

In this book on the Child Jesus, Madame Jeanne de la Mothe Guyon writes her theology of Christ's revelation in the human heart. First published in 1685, Guyon shows how God became a child to make us spiritual children. If we have a heart-felt and loving response to the Child Jesus, we become the adopted children of God and a member of the Holy Family. According to Guyon, these spiritual mysteries constitute the great gifts the Child Jesus offers us.

Madame Guyon introduces the mystery of the Child Jesus using the scripture, "If you become like a little child, you may enter the kingdom of Heaven" Matthew 18:3. Guyon understands a mystery as certain scriptures from Jesus' life that cling to us, providing us stability and virtue in life. She says the Holy Spirit chooses the appropriate mystery for us based on what we need. Guyon describes the Child Jesus as the most kind and welcoming of all the mysteries.

The Child Jesus with his inherent simplicity welcomes everyone and makes an interior home within each of us. In this mystery, we understand that the Child Jesus has a pure interior containing innocence, prayer, and abandonment. The amazing wonder is that this happy interior can also be our interior. The Child Jesus gives us this spiritual home inside and then makes us part of the Holy Family that include Mary, Joseph, and Jesus. Following this, we trust in grace, live in the will of God, and enjoy the fellowship of the Holy Family. Guyon introduces the reader to this possibility of spiritual fulfillment as she writes, "We too live as trusting children; this is the religion of the holy Child Jesus."

All of these great benefits are given to us through prayer from the heart that reaches out to the Child Jesus. When we pray, Christ creates this interior home and the Holy Spirit fills it with the character of God. Through the tenderness of this holy child, we speak openly and with familiarity to our Father who blesses our dependence on him. Through prayer, the glory and perfection of the Child Jesus fills us. Then we become content and stable, tasting already our permanent and eternal home.

Through the mystery of the Child Jesus known within, Guyon describes her distinctive theological beliefs of human abandonment and perfection. Spiritual abandonment itself is a life of complete trust and love, like a child. Guyon describes children as the most needy of creatures for they are entirely poor and naked upon entering this world. We need to become as dependent on God as every child is on other people. In our dependence, we should completely surrender to God through spiritual abandonment. Guyon states that the believer should have no self-will but be entirely indifferent to whatever human situation we are in. Indeed, our life circumstances are the ones designed by God for our spiritual growth and development. Based on the mystery of the Child Jesus, Guyon calls our life situation our cradle needed to give birth to Christ within our heart.

After giving birth to the Child Jesus, in abandonment the person finds eternity within his or her heart. Guyon defines this by saying that the abandoned person bonds entirely with God and loves God purely. After bonding with God, the person moves into an interior eternity at the speed of a quickly flowing river.

In her second distinctive idea, Guyon says that Christians live in perfection when they are abandoned. This is not a perfection achieved by gradually becoming better, but a perfection given as a gift by the Holy Spirit. When through abandonment we live with interior eyes on the Kingdom of God, a spiritual perfection fills our heart that becomes a fountain of flowing, interior peace. This spiritual fount of peace brings with it all the other virtues. The Holy Spirit gives this great gift of perfection to those bonded with God through abandonment and living in the Way of the Child Jesus.

How important are these ideas of the awakening and cleansing of the heart caused by the Child Jesus? If our hearts are cleansed within, Jesus in the Beatitudes proclaimed, "Blessed are the pure in heart, for they shall see God." With the gifts of spiritual perfection and a clean heart, we await the gift of Christ within. Guyon writes, "We want nothing except to see God. Every day we watch in every moment for God's justice and mercy along with his irreproachable wisdom." With this interior revelation of the Child Jesus, we find a spiritual fulfillment that satisfies and delights us.

In this first English translation of the Child Jesus, we see the heart of Madame Guyon's theology. To read this is to be invited into the clear depths of her spiritual thinking. We are invited to live in the mystery of the Child Jesus as we trust, love, and enjoy his grace given to us.

The Way of the Child Jesus: Our Mystery in the Heart

By Madame Jeanne de La Mothe Guyon

Dedicated to the Child Jesus

I dedicate this to you only, O very kind child and all adorable God, our small King! The Spirit designs the trust that we have in you and unites us in love to the Trinity. Your love inspires me to write. I dedicate and consecrate myself to You, who are both my origin and foundation. I depend on you.

Your arms are both the tender arms of a child and those of the all-powerful God. I have these arms as my sole protection. On you I lean. You give me the knowledge and the success that you have destined. You are my Defender, O Quiet Wisdom and Child God!

The Uncreated Word is born to us. You, a small expression of God, support us. All Christians may imitate you, for you have given your childhood to us as a model of perfection. You are in harmony with the divine original and are the excellent reflection of God. We view the eternal purposes through your full glory. You perfectly reveal the faith to those who abandon themselves to you with a perfect disinterestedness. Because we look to you and not ourselves, nothing can destroy or kill us.

The Way of the Child Jesus

Preface

Jesus welcomes us all:

The imitation of his kind, easy, and useful childhood.

We all live in this wonderful Christian order through our baptism, which makes us children of God the Father and brothers of Jesus Christ his Son. But because we leave this divine Way by our sins, or we dishonor it by our very impure lives, or violate sacred laws by our infidelities, we need to enter and connect directly with the childhood of Jesus. His childhood, the most kind of all the mysteries, brings a unique grace to us to find Christian perfection. Jesus is the powerful and complete principle, our perfect example. Because of the cleanliness of his birth in the flesh, we are born again clean in his Love.

2. In devoting ourselves to the imitation of his childhood, we enter in the spiritual order of the holy Child Jesus, and by doing this, re-enter in the true Christian Way. "Like newborn babies, long for the pure, spiritual milk, that by it you may grow up to salvation" I Peter 2:3. This order is for everyone, because the childhood of Jesus is a humble reality, and may be practiced by all kinds of people; everything is easy, lovely,

holy, pure, simple, and beautiful. It contains all possible perfection, not only on Earth but in Heaven, surpassing that of all people and all angels.

3. All sorts of people may follow this Way of Love: church leaders, laity, clergy, religious and secular. In the Child Jesus all may find both their perfection and spiritual crown. Everyone may practice this: married, celibate, judges, princes, kings, soldiers, artists, laborers, and merchants. Whether rich or poor, all will be received in the Holy Family. All will be well because the Holy Family blesses all the families of the world. Genesis 12:3 reads "All peoples on

earth will be blessed through you." Jesus came into the world for the salvation of all and to be known by all. Like the sun shines without distinction on all that are below, Jesus shines on all of us. Like the rain from heaven waters all plants, Jesus waters all of us.

4. The Gospel says this divine Way is for all and is practiced in purity and perfection. All that is asked is sweet and common. Jesus is available to all as our Savior; we see him both as example and judge. Truly, this is a marvel both admirable and infallible! The Child Jesus had both an interior and exterior. His interior opened to the eyes of God the Father; the exterior

opened to the eyes of people. Jesus had the interior of a saint and the exterior of a child: in his interior the Son of God and in the exterior the Son of Man. In the same way his Way must be distinguished in two parts: the one interior with the Spirit and the other exterior as practiced in the world.

Chapter Two

Entering into the Way:

Give yourself to Jesus Christ

1. The old Adam left the perfect Way, the original justice that God had created, and removed himself from submission to the divine will. He decided to guide himself rather than abandon himself to the Spirit of God, who was his infallible guide if he had yielded to God's Kingdom. Instead, Adam wandered and died as a criminal. Because he willed to have propriety and property opposed to God, he entered into crimes.

2. Christ, the new Adam, in contrary to this, does not live this way but gives everything to God without reservation. Without complaining, he has no will but God's; because "Then I said, 'Here I am: as it is written of me in the scroll, I have come, O God, to do your will'" Hebrews 10:7. From the first moment he served the Kingdom of God, he was perfect. He also took off propriety and was incapable of less than perfection, because he had no sin or imperfection that his own will would cause.

3. We understand that propriety brings us death and that surrender saves us. Those who want to govern themselves and be masters of

their liberty usually tend to evil because "the first inclinations of people are toward evil" Genesis 6:5. Contrary to this, God wants us to depend on Him, to be clothed with goodness, and to become more perfect. This is where the Spirit of God infallibly leads us. If we fall into a fault after yielding ourselves, we have stolen this from God because of our propriety of the will.

4. God gives us our entry into the order of Childhood and enrollment in the Holy Family. After we seriously reach for Christian perfection, if the need arises, we should confess at the time of communion. Then we must renew the infinite within as God gives inspiration, until we are in

Jesus Christ by our trusting submission. Afterwards we must stop thinking only of ourselves. We are no longer entitled to our own will in anything, but are committed to follow all divine movements. We listen in the interior to the inspirations and in the exterior we follow with obedience the guidance and providence of God.

5. The interior Spirit reveals how to unite with the Way. Nobody enters by solitary efforts, but others introduce the believer to this. For example, parents give birth and education to the dependent child. Also, Jesus Christ gives the

child the gift of the Way. He wants this predestined life for everyone.

6. Children do not know liberty and, hence, are not masters of their lives. They depend on the service of others, and they are dedicated to everything others want to do. They enter into the world in extreme dependence on their parents; they do not resist anyone and they defend nothing. We too live as trusting children; this is the religion of the holy Child Jesus.

Chapter Three

The Imitation of the Interior of the Child Jesus:

Filled with innocence, prayer and abandonment.

The interior of the Child Jesus was composed of a divine innocence, a continual prayer, and an infinite abandonment. This innocence does not have any shadow of sin and banishes all imperfection. This prayer is entirely in the spirit as a consuming perfection never interrupted by sleep or distracted by others. This abandonment is infinite and we always respond to the commands of the Father.

2. No one equals Jesus' perfection; nevertheless, all are obliged to imitate as they can, depending on the grace of God. All must strive without ceasing to the childhood of grace consisting in innocence, prayer and abandonment. We are to worship Jesus in the cradle and to observe perfectly God who is given to us all. As we read, "If you become like a little child, you may enter the kingdom of Heaven" Matthew 18:3.

Chapter Four

The Interior Purification by Penitence:

Avoid anything that displeases Jesus

The religion of the Child Jesus purifies those who imitate him from all sins by confession and by penitence. Yet will penitence, spiritual exercises, exterior work, and mortifications of the body bring a suitable childhood? A child is capable of purity, grace and love, but not rigors and austerities. The same truth applies to us. Instead, it is love that pardons sins and not harsh exercises. "Her sins, which are many, are forgiven, because she loved much" Luke 7:47. Elsewhere, we read, "Love covers a multitude of sins" I Peter 4:8. The essential and indispensable penitence happens in the interior. Indeed, the soul of all penitence is within and the exterior is only for the body. Interior penitence supports everyone. God does not ask us to do exterior penitence. Instead, He wants us to renounce sin and avoid anything that can cause sin. Then we turn our hearts to God and return to our heavenly Father. We fall with confidence into his arms. We are horrified at our crimes and know that the first inclinations of people are toward evil. After returning to God, we burn with love for God and for our neighbor. We hate injustice and follow all the commandments of God. This is a true and infallible penitence. God does not want the exterior but "the sacrifice acceptable to God is a broken spirit" and "I will not despise a contrite and humble heart" Psalm 51:17, which means, God esteems it uniquely.

2. The Child Jesus prayed in penitence for the whole world. In the bosom of his mother, in the repose of his birthplace, and during the first years of his life, he practiced this interior penitence. So also those of us who devote ourselves to Christ allow the conversion of our hearts. When our conversion leads us to work, we also change others. We then deny ourselves

the satisfactions of our own will as unnecessary: we will die to our own will and renounce our own inclinations. We will finally give up our own selfishness, after which we follow the express orders of God and the divine Way of obedience.

3. We will repent over the slightest venial sins, minor offenses, and lightest faults, because we are not willing to ever offend or displease our dear Child Jesus. Our Beloved makes a Way of Love and asks us to be forever faithful. Consequently, we have horror at even a small fault, as if it were mortal, and we guard against even a small offense. Our constant and equal

courage rejects all that might cause displeasure to him and we must through him love all things. We must no longer sin except if we are surprised and weak. By the training of our nature, we hope to commit only those sins we cannot predict well, but never ones that we understand with deliberate reflection. We have no affection for sin.

4. Nothing surpasses the grace of the Christian faith; it has been well said in the Jewish faith, "For I am the Lord your God, consecrate yourselves therefore, and be holy, for I am holy," Leviticus 11: 44. Jesus tells us, "Be you perfect, like your heavenly Father is perfect"

Matthew 5:40. Both younger and older children are filled with purity because they are not evil: and it is especially written for the lovers of the Child Jesus: "Brothers, be children, with prudence and not in malice, and be wise people" I Corinthians 14:20. We may live with the innocence of an angel under the appearance of a human being. As spiritual children, we may have a blameless heart in the eyes of our celestial Father.

5. The pure, interior innocence of children puts them out of danger of filth. By our strong interior purity, we too can avoid dangerous connections with the world. Indeed, we look at

the world as a desert for us and ask for the character of God within our hearts. When God's rest and strength reigns within, our interior state avoids and even prevents occasions for sin.

6. O we all are predestined to be the adopted children of Jesus Christ! Jesus supports us and we know that "We have been chosen before the creation of the world that we may be holy and without sin before him" Ephesians 1:4. If we live in the Way of the Child Jesus without cowardice and infidelity, we please our Beloved. We cause no harm to others. False followers love only themselves, yet they have prejudice against the true lover who loves only God. The

true lover suffers all evil to gain eternity and goes through anything to please God.

Chapter Five

The Reception of the Divine Character Within through Prayer

1. We all must pray. If we pray, we become part of the divine family. Without prayer there is no interior; prayer makes the interior, and without it you cannot be part of the family of Jesus. With an interior you can partake in the divine life of the family of Jesus, whose soul and substance rests in the interior; therefore, the principal and continual exercise of prayer brings this interior.

2. Prayer is the union of the spirit with God. This union is different, according to the different degrees of souls. (1) Some through speech and reasoning on the divine things try to raise themselves to God. This is properly called *Meditation.* (2) Some who believe hope for God, and their hearts talk to God freely. Called the *prayer of affection*, this communication lets us to rest quietly united with God. We want nothing else but to taste and enjoy the Supreme Goodness that brings happiness. This may happen through active and acquired perceptions with spiritual light. Or this may be passive and infused in an imperceptible fashion in spiritual

darkness. Both of these ways we understand as the *Prayer of Contemplation*.

3. When we pray in this true Way, the Holy Spirit, the author and director of true prayer, sweetly leads us. The will of God opens for us. Yet in prayer we scarcely know what to ask and neither do we know what is appropriate to ask. Nevertheless, "the Spirit intercedes for us with sighs too deep for words. And he who searches our hearts knows the mind of the Spirit" when we ask him to help us. Romans 8:26-27.

4. Therefore it is clear that true prayer is accomplished under the direction of the Spirit.

"Where the Spirit of the Lord is, there is freedom" 2 Corinthians 3:17. It is a useless effort to give more rules; instead, we need prayer. This is why we point to the degrees of prayer. We open our heart to the Holy Spirit, abandon to him, and move freely toward his attractions. God provides both speech and silence. We listen and ask for his grace and demand nothing but to admire and love God; to find something or perceive nothing; to be in fervor or in a drought; to be in power or weakness; to be in light or in darkness; to have consolation or desolation; to be in the mystical or in the sensible. The divine attraction speaks gently with sweetness and efficiency, and purity accompanies it. To attempt this by our own spirit is hard, diseased, twisted, sterile, insipid, and violent.

Chapter Six

Everyone Should Pray

1. Who is capable of talking to God's heart without words flowing from our mouth? We pray with both words and silence. If prayer was not meant for all, the Gospel would not say so. God exhorts us in so many places to be interior, and to speak to God within our hearts. He declares in favor of the interior. Indeed, Mary herself represents the interior. This application of the soul to God alone is "the unique necessity" and we have "chosen the better part" Luke 10:42. And the Apostle exhorts us to

pursue faith, charity, and peace found in the interior life, "with those who call on the Lord with purity of heart" 2 Timothy 2:22. Who can doubt the Apostles, disciples and the faithful women who were with their Lord in profound quiet? By his presence and grace, an excellent prayer filled their hearts.

2. Prayer with the preeminent virtues of faith, hope and love is good for all Christians. All who are baptized can form interior acts and produce them through very good and excellent prayer. Other virtuous acts fervently serving the Christian faith also depend on prayer, such as adoration, praise, contrition, petition, and

actions of grace. But where is the Christian who could produce these without a faithful heart?

3. Sadly some spiritually blind men support the idea that prayer is not for everyone and tell Christians to doubt prayer. They also blame Jesus Christ "This people honors me with their lips, but their hearts are far from me." Matthew 15:8. They teach others to do the same and obviously contradict themselves but they are enemies of eternal happiness for people. Yet "they will bear his judgment" Galatians 5:10. "Woe to those, scholars of the Law. You have taken away the key of knowledge. You yourself did not enter and you stopped those trying to

enter" Luke 11:52. They steal away from souls the treasure of Christianity, even though the Savior gives this treasure to us through his merit.

4. They could gossip and say about the Savior, "What a simple and rude man he is, talking, thinking and meeting with his friends who have left their homes. And he cannot do this with God present!" Don't they know that God sees the sentiments in their hearts and yet they are not expressing truthful words with their mouths? All they say are absurdities! We know that "God tests hearts and minds" Psalms 7:9. Also, "The Lord hears the desire of the poor and

listens to the thoughts of their hearts" Psalms 10:17. Yet do the false scholars speak God's words with their mouth? Who is the patient who does not uncover his wounds to the doctor, to see what has to be done to heal? Who is the poor person who would rather starve and die rather than reach out to a rich person and open the door to receive help? Doesn't a servant remain for some time in silence and repose before the Master, waiting upon his orders? Doesn't a friend talk with his friend? Or doesn't a child wait upon the father so they can speak or hug him? Like these relationships when we pray, we talk sweetly with God heart-to-heart. Even though there are certain differences between prayers of the spirit and those of the mouth, there is communication between the soul and the body, between the heart and the word, and between the order of the divine and the order of the natural. Some humans can be content with appearances and expressions spoken from the mouth but God mainly looks at the heart. "I do not judge things," God says, "as humans judge" because "people see outside appearances but the Lord looks into the heart" I Samuel 16:7.

5. O my Brother! O my Sister! All should have the habit of Prayer. You say the "Our Father" yet is it enough only to say the words?

Uttered by the mouth, each of its requests contains plenty for a good, long, and fervent meditation or contemplation: and repentance penetrates vividly the bottom of the heart, producing many good effects. This experience you understand well and, if you ponder it all day, you find you change into another person. For this profound prayer attracts for you the spirit of God that brings this admirable change. "The Spirit of the Lord will come upon you" and you will change into a different person, as described in I Samuel 10:6. This promise extends to all people through prayer.

6. You call God our Father and put this sweet name at the beginning of this unique and universal prayer. Finally, without fear you will see, that God has you as a friend and ally in a brotherly trust. It is not necessary to prepare, study and arrange for discourse to speak with him, but like a son who never fails to speak to his father. They use language easily one-to-another, and it might appear too familiar to another. However, this is the best way for children to speak to their fathers.

7. O all you who wish to be disciples in the school of Bethlehem, allies with Jesus Christ! Speak to him from your heart with familiar

language, and express your preference in a simple prayer. "I pour out my complaint before him" Psalm 142:2. You will discover confidence in your troubles; and you by grace will see that God is kind. Like the Shepherds and Wise Men, who adored Jesus in the manger, we speak openly with him.

Chapter Seven

The Practice of Beginning, Advanced, and Passive Prayer

The Child Jesus is for everyone. Anyone practicing this must yield and be led by the Holy Spirit, without any resistance, and hope to discover the divine attraction and leadership.

2. If you want to pray and close the gap between you and God, turn a blind eyes to things outside and call forth the strength within you. Put yourself in the presence of God by recollecting that he is for everyone "and in

particular lives in your heart." Give yourself to Jesus Christ so that he is in your prayer, imploring him to "teach us to pray" Luke 11:1: all of him and nothing of you. Pray then abandoned to him, following the attractiveness of his grace with all its freedom.

3. Do not search for God outside of yourself, in heaven or in images, or in any other place, but search inside you where he truly lives. "If you love me," he said, "you will keep my word, and my Father will love you, and we will come to you, and make our home with you" John 14:23. Why seek for God far away if he is within all of us? Or why be in anxiety and

worry, when he can be discovered in love in the bottom of our heart? O inestimable happiness that at all hours we can converse with him in any time or place, in any state or situation! When we discover this interior door opening to the Lord's joy, we find the hidden treasure of the gospel. Our faith asks us to keep company with this divine guest who brings spiritual well being.

4. After beginning prayer, we must never stop because he pours himself into our heart in our time and continues there, even while we work. Nothing prevents this work if you guard your silence in prayer and divine exercises in your certain hours consecrated to God. Never be

discouraged by the pain that you find. Prayer is at its best when yielding to the cross of Jesus Christ who blesses all spiritual works crucified and abandoned to him. If you believe you have lost everything, suddenly everything reverses and "your life will be brighter than the noonday" Job 11:17. Do not be eager for sweetness and consolation: if God gives this to you, receive this with humility, and remain united to him and occupied only with him. Banish any complaints about your prayer and instead bless God for giving his generous grace. For if you remain in God's presence, and give loving looks to his Divine Majesty, you will have an inestimable reward and that alone will reward infinitely all the hours that you have sought him.

5. We all recognize that we have distractions. When these nuisances happen in his presence, and we painfully suffer, look at the Divine Majesty with love. This is invaluable. When with patience we spend hours with him, we can be free of distractions. Even if the heart is focused while the spirit distracted, we remain united with God during this and persist in the divine will to pray. We do not force ourselves or act contrarily; instead, we use this for our advantage by treating this distraction with

contempt and do not even regard it and we turn to look again at God.

6. We remain open to whatever we hear in prayer will please God. His will gives us a strong character with constant contentment. Walk in faith and with abandon, and assuredly we will have fruits from prayer that are infinite. These fruits are principally not known in this life but are reserved for the beautiful day of eternity.

7. The spirit of prayer carries us through the day, while we remain in the same mood or disposition. We seek God frequently and, leaving the exterior, we recollect ourselves in the

interior and think about, speak to, and listen to God. Waiting for holy inspiration with loving looks, fervent prayer, and affectionate thoughts, we value the spiritual world. We give all to God, as much as our occupation permits.

8. We may easily practice this in the midst of our employment without fatigue; artists, laborers, and managers are very capable of this. We direct all our hearts, indeed all our energies to God, so we may find faith and love in our experience. In God we find Jesus, Mary and Joseph and apply this interiorly so that while we work, we live in the hands of the divine family.

9. In this infallible manner of excellent prayer, we speak openly and freely with God. To speak spiritually with God shows our tender union. Even beginners may follow the movement of the Holy Spirit. At the beginning in prayer we always spend a part of the time in our interior silently before God. "Happy are those who dwell in your house! They never cease to praise you" Psalm 84:5. We listen to what God says and follow his attractions. We do this because the continual Babel of the creature hurts the operations of God and destroys the interior place of divine inspiration.

10. Without reservation we advance in abandonment to God by following the divine attractions with faithfulness and allowing the full actions of God, without willing or knowing. We remain in silence and repose at the feet of the Lord, focusing on him only. We find contentment in admiring and loving him, that we may not be tired in the multiple work of Martha, but may have the joy of the better part of Mary. By our extreme humility through keeping God in sight, we may be capable of receiving God, so that finally through our own nothingness we may have a place in infinity with God. It is through this way of remaining

attached to God only that we become "one Spirit with the Lord" 1 Corinthians 6:17.

11. Those who are called to supernatural prayer and passive reception carry the name of the Holy Family, where they remain without resistance, because here are the eminent people, Joseph, Mary, and Jesus. We do not fear from any of the critical words we hear and we ignore any condemning thoughts from others. When we become advanced, we discern easily any difficulties with others and understand how God is glorified. It is right to be pure in his Spirit, for those "who are led by the Spirit of God are sons

of God" Romans 8:14. We yield to the operations of God.

12. The soul in this passive state finds reason, peace, and stability, and has the mark of a real and excellent operation of God. Then the soul finds happiness, and, while this is mystical, yet the soul creates fruits in the material world. We love and possess the Sovereign Good through faith in an unknown but very real manner. We taste, know and love those divine things more than others, even in the world's vast nothingness, profound obscurity and open fright. We see only the Sovereign Good that causes repose, satisfaction, peace, and stability.

But this light is hidden "under a bushel" Luke 11:33 except to those who lose their life. Are we astonished if it is unknown to those who do not have the experience?

Chapter Eight

Praying Freely with Affection

If we really understand that God is present, we can talk to him with our heart. "My God, I adore you. I believe in your word; I hope in your mercy; I love your goodness and I regret having offended you; I am deformed but supported by your grace. I renounce all sins and will constantly avoid occasions for sin; I accept with penitence that I will please your justice through suffering. You help me pray excellently, and you continue to move inside of me." We also pray like those holy people that the Scriptures give to us as examples.

2. If we look at the spirit of Jesus crucified, we will find him approachable, "My Lord and my God! It is for me that you suffered death on the cross! In you I have mercy with all your saints that are found in you! Cleanse me, my sweet Savior, from all my sins in your blood! Save me through the price of your death! Help me through grace not to offend, because my sins caused you to suffer torments! Let me suffer for your love, O adorable Love, because you have suffered for me! I accept all the blows of your love." And we pray without reason or

phoniness; only the cross of Jesus is a model achievement of prayer.

3. If we desire to advance in perfection, we pray in this way profoundly in our soul. "O Jesus, my divine Master! Help me renounce myself and carry my cross with you very day as I follow you: let me conform entirely to your will! Make me as you please; I give myself to you without reservation, renouncing everything without taking anything back; I abandon everything to your pleasure; make me walk in your ways that I always remember my God, and live in the loving ways of the Beloved of my soul! You, O my God, the God of my heart and

my portion forever!" Psalm 73: 26. This prayer purifies us for eternity and ravishes the heart of God; this disengages us from the creature and attaches us only to the Lord for the Spirit shows many things, but only affection of the heart makes the soul fly to God.

4. With a spiritually strong heart, we find frequent sweet pleasures. For example, "O God, that I know you and that I know myself!" St. Augustine. "O my God and my all!" St. Francis. "You are all that is, there is nothing but you." "The Lord is good, his mercy is everlasting." "Your will makes the earth like heaven" Matthew 6:10. You speak, and our memory

repeats, that in you we have satisfaction. Remaining in you, God gives us the fire of God that raises us up. We follow you with a humble and impetuous spirit because in prayer we remember David, Augustine, Francis and all the holy saints.

5. All Christians can pray and the Church teaches its children how to pray. The Spirit of grace prays in yielded hearts. We collect fruits in this way of prayer, bringing before God hundreds or thousands of concerns and works. In the same Spirit of the Son of God, we pray for strength like true children. Scripture testifies about our Father. "The Spirit of the Son in our

hearts makes us cry, 'Abba! Father!'" Galatians 4:6. In this charming cry full of simplicity and innocence, we see the character of the Son's prayer and we become like the adopted children and brothers of Jesus Christ, when we speak the same in our interior, "My Lord and my God!" John 20:28. "Abba! Father!" Mark 14:36. "My Father who art in heaven! My Jesus! My Savior, my kind Redeemer, who I know! I obey you! I serve you! I love you! I am yours forever!" This worthy prayer goes through the Son to the Father, and this worthy offering goes through the Spirit to God the Father: and all this is easy because the Son of Man is capable.

Don't we pity those who do not know how to pray? And do some still pretend that mental prayer is not for everyone?

Chapter Nine

The Advantages and Ease of Abandonment

We must go through darkness in order to learn to be entirely led by God. All Christians are exhorted by the Holy Spirit to abandon ourselves because as he says, "Do not worry about tomorrow" for "your heavenly Father knows what you need" Matthew 6:32, 34. And also, "Cast all your anxieties on him, for he cares about you" I Peter 5:7. Because of these scriptures, it is appropriate that the child of grace be entirely abandoned because a child does not have worries but has faith. He does not worry about the past or the future. He or she lives in simplicity in the present moment, very indifferent about what to do.

2. The children of Jesus practicing abandon live distinctively. Therefore the practice is (1) to lose our own will and to live in God's will: and renounce all inclination, particularly the natural ones that appear good, but to be in indifference, and to will only for God and eternity. (2) To be indifferent to all things, whether for the body or the soul, or in time or eternal. (3) Leave the past forgotten and the future to providence, we give the present to God and live content in the actual moment because

the eternal Way of God works for us. We are the infallible declaration of the will of God as it is meant and inevitable for all. (4) We do not think of anything as from human beings but all things are from God and we receive everything as from God's hand to save us from our sins.

3. The children of grace are content with faith and abandon. We walk safely in a community without extraordinary ambition, delightful feelings, or sublime lights. We depend on God alone. Pretending nothing, we do not stop to examine ourselves. But through generous abandon, we run toward God without fatigue and without stopping on the way. We

reach for the Sovereign Good, while knowing that God will give a perfect repose.

4. Having learned from God about the life of faith and pure love, we receive with stability everything given to us from moment to moment: light or darkness, ease or difficulty, strength or weakness, vigor or illness, sweetness or bitterness. Even temptations, distractions, and scruples do not stop us because our faithful abandon destroys them. We want nothing except to see God. Every day we watch in every moment for God's justice and mercy along with his irreproachable wisdom.

5. But to live this way, we must be abandoned and follow the grace given to us. Then we become a holy Child who does not idolize other things. We do not have resistance, repugnance, hesitation, narrow-mindedness, or defensiveness. If we are entirely on fire for God, we avoid temptations. We see that we have a share reserved for us in the divine kingdom. Because of this, we must practice this movement to God wherever we are. To the degree where God discovers the soul in its new abandon, God blesses us. We cannot pretend a faithful abandon to God because how can we pretend our bonding with God alone? We find support in God's will and judgment that makes

our faith and connection to God strong. We believe that God does see and keeps us in his will; then we have no other judgment or will but the will of God.

6. A true abandonment makes us strong and repulses sin. For it is written, "We know that any one born of God does not sin, but He who was born of God keeps him, and the evil one does not touch him" I John 5:18. How can we sin when we remain in the hands of God, and we do not leave? We remain inspired by God. Yet if we sin, we return to God and abandon ourselves in faithfulness. We lose ourselves in the heart of God and taste God's healing power. If we become defiant, we injure

ourselves because we think it dangerous to abandon ourselves to God and do not trust God's goodness.

7. When we abandon ourselves, we give honor to God; in abandonment we offer an excellent praise to our Creator and his ways and ends. For we then offer perfect religion and exacting justice to our Sovereign King. He loves with a pure love and because of this, we can love him with above all things and more than self. We love with true generosity and purity. It is worshipping the "Father in spirit and truth" John 4:23: in spirit, above all natural knowledge and in truth, above our own self-interest. It is the "your will be done, on earth, as it is in

heaven" Matthew 6:10. By honoring God through an infinite abandonment, the Son of God becomes a child to us: and with an increasing honor, we live in this childhood. The Child Jesus gives grace for us to walk in this premier way.

8. Following this way, we do not have complaints, impatience or murmuring. Even troubles are fine to us: the states of being lost, poor, and sick do not shake us. Even death does not frighten us. "The wisdom of God is justified by all her children" Luke 7:35. We do not fear anymore the evils of this life, because a child does not fear dwelling in his cradle.

9. One thing is known: stability is easy when we see and know the will of God. We discover this in all experiences, both when we are strong and in pain. All life we search for the will of God and accomplish this because God is near to us. We live in the present moment without looking to the past and not worrying about the future. The will of God allows us to live in each instant. This is the way to find God and to reconnect to his easy way of life for it is God who makes this.

When we have the Child Jesus in our interior, we live in him and realize his desire to be made present in our exterior.

Chapter Ten

The Exterior of the Childhood of Jesus:

A Confident and Sincere Dependence

The brothers and sisters of the Child Jesus imitate the exterior of his childhood. He appeared humble yet with justice, perfection and the dignity of God. He had no corruption or impurity. In the same way, the exterior of his brothers and sisters must also humbly follow their vocation with nothing contrary to God. We are also free from all disorder because holiness does not consist in things extraordinary or brilliant but in justice and righteousness. The children of God do not seek to be admired by human beings, but to be pleasing to the eyes of their heavenly Father.

2. The childhood of Jesus was passed in basic simplicity and dependence because when very small a child cannot talk or walk. It is powerless to make choices. After all, who is simpler than a child who cannot say their thoughts and who has no disguise for natural instincts? And who is more dependent than a child who does not resist anything asked from him? Indeed, the character of the child of grace is basic simplicity and dependence.

3. To be simple is a love of abjection and a quiet acquiescence to all humiliations of Providence. To live in simplicity is to be content to have "the lowest place" Luke 14:10 without ambition for the grand graces or to be lifted up or to practice strong austerities or to be high in the church; but to be content in all poverty and nakedness, that are the natural states of childhood, resting naturally in the cradle. Divine Providence has prepared our share of knowledge, state, vocation, and talents. Without having grand designs, we are truly conformed to the Child Jesus.

4. Simplicity is a correspondence of the heart with all that is exterior: in strength we

speak like we think and we think like we speak and we act like we think. In short, we have integrity as the simple "children of God" Galatians 3:26. We avoid disguise, phoniness, pretense, exaggeration, flattery, contempt, and arrogance that the corrupted Spirit of the world invents for the work of malicious people. Therefore the small innocents are incapable of this century's corruption and the prudence of the flesh. The world admires intrigue and politics, false affections, the spirit of power, and false reasoning. Holy people reject this so they may abandon to the Wisdom of God.

5. We exercise dependence by obedience, which is the appropriate character for children of

grace. For the Child Jesus has holy parents and he does nothing except by their movement; we see the King of glory obedient to his parents. In the same way, the friends of the manger must be obedient people. We obey our superiors in the church without excuse or delay. We apply our heart and spirit to our work with all affection and believing without hesitation that God is in the middle of this, and that this is the will of God declared to us. This is perfect obedience.

6. Frequently we repent in our hearts, and observe in our conduct the example of Jesus' love; we are submissive to his love, which is the point of the true child who is obedient and submissive to his parents.

Chapter Eleven

The Character of the Children of the Holy Family

We do not distinguish the Holy Family's children by their exterior appearance but by their interior peace. This spiritual peace carries their works and virtues.

In contrast to the children of the Holy Family, the children of the world want their mansions, habits, lives, and ceremonies. The children of the Holy Family are indifferent to everything except the Kingdom of Jesus. In interior Christians we see modesty, silence and recollection. We know them by their peace and sweetness, their charity and support of one another. We know them by their righteousness and integrity in life. In kindness they contribute one to another. All of these qualities are known as the reign of Jesus, our King of Kings.

2. Our union with this adorable family calls us to look everywhere for the grand glory of God and to seek perfection in our spiritual work. The spirit of Jesus is both a universal and a particular spirit. Through this unique and multiplying spirit as described in Wisdom 7:12-30, a pastor in the Church fulfills his ministry with dignity; a prince governs his state with holiness; a judge gives justice to all with

integrity; a business person negotiates with honesty; an artist toils with perseverance; a soldier engages in combat with service to the general; neither the noise of war nor the heat of combat stops us from doing everything for God. Courageously we persevere. Because we love God with all our heart, we will not be afraid, for our love carries a lively confidence in God. We work for others and guard our duty faithfully because of our Sovereign God. We serve others because as we do this we, "willingly serve the Lord" Ephesians 6:7. For example, a wife and husband care for their duties and children. Spiritual parents make their families happy, for they rule their own conduct with the example of

Mary and Joseph, while the children have as an example Jesus.

3. All carry in our heart cooperation with the divine Way as we guard the indestructible *peace* that announced the birth of our Savior to people of good will. Our peace cannot be altered because we want nothing except what is given to us from moment to moment. We want to lose everything for the divine will; we want only his will. We can face any difficulty because Jesus' heart helps us accept everything planned for us. We don't doubt the care of his arms.

Our future promises us peace because Jesus is there. We do not take our strength and comfort from the world. Avoiding any dishonesty, we receive everything from the hands of God. Our well-being signals the divine goodness. God puts far away from us chagrin and gives us excellent actions of grace. In the spirit of abandonment, we practice the wisdom of the Gospels. We regard everything as the actions of God and attribute nothing to the creature. Receiving everything equally from the goodness of our Creator, we do not judge the success of our enterprise according to people's petty reasoning by an apparent advantage or an action's consequence. But we believe that the true success of all things is in the glory and order of God, for we are hidden in him in the day of

Eternity. God does not judge by human appearances or understanding and so we peacefully remain in God.

Chapter Twelve

Spiritual Exercises to Help the Exterior

As members of the Holy Family, we offer all our days to the Lord and spend all our hours regally. We fulfill all our duties faithfully and, because of this, we have a good order in their home. We hear the divine whispers all our days. Our Lord rewards our faith with time filled with the light of understanding. The effect is amazing.

2. Pray three times a day for the honor of the loving Trinity and the three persons of the sacred family. This strengthens our power and

gives us freedom. This raises us up. On these three people of Mary, Joseph, and Jesus, we relax like a couch. Our time, situation and state decide the length of our prayer. Sometimes we pray for an hour or part of an hour; other times we have a quarter of an hour or even take a minute during the day. Our responsibilities and the degree of our interiority decide whether we pray vocally. We pray continually from our heart, yet we do not speak many prayers.

3. We read spiritual literature every day and find this indispensable. If we take a few moments for nurture, we find this an excellent way to help our spoken words. In reading we receive advice and wisdom. All our days we

work with our hands, as we exercise charity for others; we observe that other dignified persons of quality do the same.

4. Offering prayer minute to minute in ordinary life intensifies our powers if done frequently. This honors the mystery of the Incarnation and the birth of our Savior. When we do this, we imitate the early Christians who had seen the Apostles and lived like them.

5. The fifth day of each month are for us solemn days. We will fast for one day and one additional hour for 25 hours. Without fail we will take communion that day.

6. We take the Eucharist frequently. Like children, we live in the manger and eat the bread of Bethlehem, who is Jesus the Son of God. Jesus brings the bread of Angels in heaven and gives bread to the people born children on earth.

7. All our life we confess to God in the manner in which we are capable. The most appropriate time is Advent in which we have a grand silence to honor the eternal Word, hidden and quiet in the bosom of Mary. We may eat or fast, or be abstinent during our time, that we may honor the Child Jesus, true source of all graces.

8. We all comprehend these faithful exercises, so that we may also offer in the church our particular faithful testimony to the Child Jesus. We also yield to the Mother of our King. Our testimony makes us ready to shed our blood in the work of the Child Jesus and to receive his help for the growth of all our gifts. We obey without resistance all his orders.

9. We cannot speak of our Holy Family at corrupt and dissolute entertainments, for these lack dignity for Christians. We renounce these. In any undignified activities, how could the brothers and sisters of the Child Jesus be the flower of Christianity? Instead, women renounce all immodesty and nudity for if they

adopt impure vanity, they renounce the divine Way. According to our condition, we bring virtue and honor without pretense and negligence, so we do not look ridiculous but like model Christians.

10. We use all of our energy for works, both physical and spiritual, to return to others the Son of God's mercy to us.

Chapter Thirteen

The Physical Works of Mercy

The rich must give abundant alms. Nothing will exempt us from giving help and the work of our hands in service to the poor, because it is written for us, "The point is this: he who sows sparingly will also reap sparingly, and he who sows bountifully will also reap bountifully. Each of you must do as he has made up his mind, not reluctantly or under compulsion, for God loves a cheerful giver" 2 Corinthians 9: 6-7.

2. People with the needed authority should establish hospitals and charities for the relief of the poor. They also found churches offering strong and continual charity for the poor. These will bring infinite fruit throughout eternity. The churches provide simple and easy remedies, so they are signs of *Medicine for the Poor*. They provide a refreshing drink of faith and trust in Providence. This makes every day full of miracles meeting the needs of the neglected poor. We become the watchmen looking for cures for poverty.

3. Everyone who loves Jesus Christ loves the poor: and anyone who does not love the poor does not love Jesus Christ. O you who

profess a tender devotion to the Child Jesus: remember to have a tender compassion for the poor, and every hour give prompt and holy assistance for the relief of the poor. "Yet for your sake he became poor, so that by his poverty you might become rich" 2 Corinthians 8:9.

4. Never refuse a poor person who is presented to you. Go in search of them if they do not present themselves. Visit anyone in need. Meet all afflictions with strong assistance for the love of Jesus, that you may not refuse his blood that is necessary to save you.

I. Smit fec.

Chapter Fourteen

The Spiritual Works of Mercy: Prayer that Reveals the Interior and Exterior of Jesus. An Exhortation to the Interior Prayer of the Heart

Pastors in the church make known to others the knowledge of the reign of Jesus Christ in souls, because it is there that our truthful and sovereign King desires to rule. This way of prayer develops both an interior and exterior that reveals God's reign.

2. If we work for the conversion of souls, we will win the hearts, and through prayer, make infinite and durable conversions. But when we focus on the exterior and teach many precepts for behavior, the souls will bear little fruit and the conversion will not last long.

3. When ministers have zeal to instruct parishioners, these shepherds guard their people and give them the Holy Spirit. The people are then led and ablaze with the Spirit and bear eternal fruit; their vices are banished and they become spiritual. They stop blasphemies, curses, hatred, crimes, and debaucheries; they reign as dignified people. Jesus rules peacefully for all and the church renews its rule in all places.

Through the loss of the interior, heresies enter into the world; if the interior is established, destruction stops while the church is restored.

4. O terrible loss if the interior is neglected! Oh what an accounting church leaders will have to give if they have not fulfilled their duty to instruct about the treasure of the Word hidden in the cradle of the Son! How can we ever repay this if we fail to let others know of eternity within? How can we repay if we have taken away the glory of God and the merits of souls from those for whom we are responsible?

5. Some think that this is a dangerous road and that simple people are not capable of

spiritual matters. But there is no danger in walking in the sight of Jesus Christ and giving everything to him, to look at him without ceasing, placing all our trust in his grace, and placing all our powers in his pure love. And far from the idea that simple are not capable of this, they are more appropriate for this because they are docile, humble, and innocent. They are not attached to their own understanding and because of this, they move easily with the Spirit of God, depending on him for their subsistence, unlike those who are blinded by their things and resist the Spirit. Also, God has declared, "The upright are in the Lord's confidence" Proverbs

3:32. Also, we read, "The Lord, my strength and might, came to me as savior" Psalm 118: 14.

6. Also, the Father of souls warns, "For my people have committed two evils: they have forsaken me, the fountain of living waters, and hewed out cisterns for themselves, broken cisterns that can hold no water" Jeremiah 2:13. Remember to hold fast to Jesus, the fountain of living water. We apply this remedy to the evil in the heart. By welcoming the Child Jesus to our interior, we take away our preoccupation with the exterior that is like the wind. But if we give away the key to the interior, the exterior becomes everything. Yet the interior is easy; search for God within our hearts and think

about him. Return to him when distracted, and allow his plans in order to please him. This is how to find his grace and our increasing spiritual growth.

7. We are committed to help everyone place Jesus Christ in view. His blood has been shed for our souls. "Speak tenderly to Jerusalem!" Isaiah 40:2. Dispensators of these graces! O ministers of the sacraments! O Preachers of the Word! Establish his Kingdom so that he truly reigns in the hearts because it is the heart only that can be opposed to his kingdom. Likewise, it is the affection of the heart that honors the Kingdom.

8. Make a catechism that teaches prayer, not reasoning or methods of which simple people are not capable; but a *Prayer of the Heart* and not the mind; a *Prayer of Love* and not speculation; a *Prayer of the Spirit of God* and not the spirit of humanity. Alas, we make magnificent prayers and try too hard and make prayer impossible! But the Spirit of God is beyond these prayers. God is pleased when shepherds become prophets and live far away from palaces and not with some Christians, who full of imagination, live contrary to the open door of God. Wisdom of God cries to all in the public places "Whoever is simple, let him turn in here!" Proverbs 9:4.

9. We understand that the ancient truths provide the best support but they are hidden under our forgetfulness of ancient truths. The ancient authors testify to prayer for we can only pray with our whole heart. The simple children of God have the experience and knowledge; they are interior and their methods of prayer are the ancient ones of the Church. Angels gave these early graces to human beings, because these graces raise us to God and unite us freely to the Holy Spirit.

10. The leaders and pastors who depend on God by nourishing and reforming produce missions in their places. Therefore, the blessings of God accompany them. The religious who

apply their hearts to this are happy to be part of the Kingdom of Jesus and find great advantage in reigning with him and joining their souls in prayer.

11. Finally, the Child Jesus asks us to adore him in his cradle and he will open our hearts to devotion in the interior life where we will receive faith and love. We see him without distraction and offer gifts to him unceasingly. We form the habit of receiving the loving gaze of God that fills us and contains all actions and virtues. Whatever happens we give all gifts to him and not to ourselves. We remain strong in the state of giving. O if we may lose all our propriety, we will resemble God, because we are

nourished and united with God! O if we can remain entirely with him and not worry about ourselves but think by faith of the Child Jesus, we approach his perfection! His childhood gives grace for us to be conformed to his heart.

12. Therefore remain with this kind King; be with him without reservation; agree to him without resistance. O Love! You are kind and humble and we wish to imitate you. Give us your invincible graces! An infinite number of people love you and imitate you in the charm and perfection of your childhood!

Those who follow this way will find excellent spiritual growth and they will take

Love into their lives through the reading of this book.

Selected Bibliography

Guyon, Jeanne. 1717. *Ame Amante de son Dieu, representée dans les emblems de Hermannus Hugo sur ses pieux desirs: & dans ceux d'Othon Vaenius sur l'amour divin. Avec des figures nouvelles acompangées de vers qui en font l'aplication aux dispositions les plus essential*. Cologne: Jean de la Pierre.

_____. 1685. *Regle des associes a l'enfance de Jesus, modele de perfection pour tous les estates, tire de la Sainte Ecriture et des Peres*. Lyon.

James, Nancy Carol. 2011. *The Complete Madame Guyon*. Massachusetts: Paraclete Press.

_____. 1998. *The Apophatic Mysticism of Madame Guyon*. Michigan: UMI Dissertation Services.

_____. 2014. *I, Jeanne Guyon*. Florida: Christian Books Publishing House.

_____. 2007. *The Pure Love of Madame Guyon*. Lanham, Maryland: University Press of America.

———. 2014. *The Soul, Lover of God: Emblems by Madame Guyon and Herman Hugo*. Lanham, Maryland: University Press of America.

James, Nancy Carol and Sharon D. Voros. 2012. *Bastille Witness: the Prison Autobiography of Madame Guyon (1648-1717)*. Lanham, Maryland: University Press of America.

James, William. 2004. *The Varieties of Religious Experience*. New York: Barnes & Noble Classics.

Veen, Otto van. 1615. *Amoris Divini Emblemata*. Anvers.